HEARTBEATS

OF THE HOLY

A Philosophy of Ministry

HEARTBEATS
OF THE HOLY

A Philosophy of Ministry

by Keith E. Knauss

Faithful Life Publishers
North Fort Myers, FL 33903

www.FLPublishers.com

Heartbeats of the Holy

Copyright © 2009

ISBN: 978-0-9821408-7-1

Published, printed, and distributed by:
Faithful Life Publishers
3335 Galaxy Way
North Fort Myers, FL 33903

www.FLPublishers.com

Previously published by Fundamental Baptist Fellowship International,
2801 Wade Hampton Blvd. • Suite 115-165 • Taylors, SC 29687
www.fbfi.org • (864) 268-0777 • Frontline Magazine (journal of FBFI)
and printed by Mission Graphics of Westland, MI 48185

Scripture quotations are from the King James Version

Printed in the United States of America

17   16   15   14   13   12   11   10   09   2 3 4 5 6

DEDICATED

to

*The Exaltation
of the Savior
and
The Encouragement
of His Servants*

CONTENTS

INTRODUCTION

What a moment that was when the blessed Holy Spirit, moved with infinite compassion, reached down and gathered up this sin-stricken world in His arms and brooded over it with unspeakable burden. That burden for a dying world has not passed away; it has been passed on, in a measure, to those who have felt the calling hand of God strong upon them.

Holy men of God have come walking bowed beneath the immeasurable weight of the Divine Word and a Demanding Work. They have come treading through the tumult of their times, the voice of One crying in the wilderness. Such men have been declared the offscouring of a world unworthy of them, pouring out upon their own hearts a loathsome load of contempt and condemnation at their own unworthiness and unfitness. John felt such personal unworthiness as he strode through the wilderness pointing men to the Lamb of God. That loin-clad evangelist came with the sweet taste of honey in his mouth, but the sound of Divine authority in his voice; all the while confessing himself unworthy to so much as stoop down and unloose the latchet of the shoes of his Lord.

Great is the burden of that holy calling, and great are the consequences of neglecting it. It is an unceasing Gethsemane that besets the heart and mind and soul of one so privileged to stand before men in the stead of God. Paul experienced this and said, "Woe is me if I preach not the Gospel." Saintly Alexander Whyte expressed that fearful feeling, when he spoke the tumult of the pastor-heart, "Oh, my brethren, the never-to-be-redeemed opportunities of our pulpits; and the lasting blame of God, and our people, and of our own consciences, for the misuse and neglect of our pulpits! Rock of Ages, cleft for ministers!"

May the gracious Holy Sprit be pleased to take this presentation of thought gathered from holy men of God both past and present and capture their heartbeat for us. May He see fit to stir the fires within our hearts and renew our determination to magnify our office, to give ourselves up to God's work, to labor in season and out, to do good and give no offense that both the ministry and ourselves be lifted up above all fault-finding of fair-minded men.

Keith E. Knauss

1 CALLING AND COMPULSION

The call of the Eternal must ring through the corridors of a man's soul as clearly as the sound of the morning alarm bell calls men to their labors. The circumstances may differ but the call is just as definite.

There is Amos, a poor herdsman, brooding deeply and solitarily amid the thin pastures of Tekoa. Rumors come his way of dark doings in high places. Wealth is breeding prodigality. Luxury is producing callousness. Injustice is rampant. Truth is fallen in the streets. As Amos mused, "the fire burned," and out on those lone wastes he heard a mysterious call and saw a beckoning hand. For him there was no alternative: "The Lord took me as I followed the flock, and said, Go, prophesy!"

We cannot tell how that call will come to us, or what will be the manner of its coming. It may be that the Divine constraint will be as soft and gentle as a glance. It may be that constraint will seize us with a strong and invisible grasp, as though we were in the custody of an iron hand from which we cannot escape. Isaiah wrote, "The Lord said unto me with a strong hand. " The call of God laid hold of Isaiah with a strong grip that imprisoned him like a vice. He was carried along by divine coercion. Like Paul, "necessity was laid" upon him. He was in bonds and must obey.

It is doubtful if God regards any calling on earth as higher or more sacred than that of the ministry. Henry Ward Beecher said, in a lecture to students at Yale, "God stands at the door of the womb of nature and calls men to birth. When a quarter of a man is born He says, 'Stand aside!' When a half man is born He again says, 'Stand aside!' When three quarters of a man is born He still says, 'Stand aside!' But when a whole man is born God says, 'Come forth; here is my preacher!' "

Look at the titles God dignifies His preachers with. They are called Messengers, Watchmen, Workmen, Witnesses, Teachers, Pastors, Shepherds, Evangelists, Ministers, Stewards, Prophets, Ambassadors, etc. Ministers ought to feel the peculiar dignity and immeasurable importance of their work and calling, and magnify their office and make it honorable.

"No man taketh this honor unto himself, but he that is called of God" (Hebrews 5:4). No ambassador appoints himself to represent his country at a foreign court. He is invited by the President or King or Emperor. So a man must wait for God's call to preach. A mere desire to preach for the respectability of it, or the publicity or notoriety of it, is simply contemptible. "How shall they preach except they be sent?"

Our Lord did not call soft-palmed, lily-fingered sons of pleasure to herald His saving message. He went down to the sea and called some brawny-muscled, horny-handed fishermen, used to pulling oars in the teeth of the fierce storms of Gennesaret. God called men who were real men.

Think of Paul. He may have been small in stature, but he was huge in heart. Check the astonishing list of things he endured (II Cor. 11:23-28). After naming twenty three incredible experiences, as if they were not enough, Paul added, "Besides those things . . . the care of ALL the churches!" That was a load greater than any reed shaken by wind could possibly endure. Yet with the weight of all the churches upon him, Paul still had the vitality to trudge along the Appian Way to Rome with fire in his eyes and conquest in his soul, and make himself such a terror to evil doers that the devil had to kill him to get rid of that all-conquering personality.

Think of that man called Martin Luther, whose words were fiery swords, who trod the field of his age like an armoured giant, the sound of whose footfall was heard in Rome, and made popes tremble! The magnetic influence of his masterful life is still marching on like an army with banners. Then, as always, God had His men hand-picked, and they moved onward with the awesome awareness of Divine calling and compulsion.

2 PREACHER AND PULPIT

The preacher has more to do with the spirit of the ages than with the spirit of the age. A preacher must not be engulfed in the NOW. He hears the reverberations of all the waves that ever beat upon the shores of human history. He embraces all time. He is blood relative to the divinities in time and eternity.

The lure of preaching is the lure of exploits and accomplishments, and if the preaching of the Gospel is not utterly necessary, it is utterly unnecessary. Except a man's ministry be momentous, he himself is trivial.

Never lose the wonder of preaching! Preach with that wonder in your voice. Walk through this realm of marvel with the wonder-wind fanning your face. Thou are kinsman of this land of God, this Beulah land where the beatitudes forever fall. Preacher, you ever live on the edge of miracles. Our God can make dry bones to live. Don't become a dry bone with the wonder all gone.

Preachers are men of meditation. We are kinsmen of the skies. We wear this heavenly atmosphere. We tramp along kindling splendors of the Almighty and feel no burning of our bare feet in tramping through those fires. For such goings we were meant. "Behold, this dreamer cometh" was said in derision by the brothers of Joseph. But Joseph's dream became purveyor to Egypt and saviour to those witless brethren. That dreamer was the revealer and distributor of bread.

Preaching that does not make heaven richer and hell poorer is not worthy of the name. Whoever would be successful as a fisher of men must shape his sermons to that end. He must descend from the brilliant generalizations of truth which everybody can assent to with delight, and come down to particulars, and make the text a "thus saith the Lord" to the individual conscience and heart.

Let the ambassador, through whose lips the living God speaks to dying men, be awake to the situation. He may have perhaps forty minutes to arouse an audience from the stupefaction of worldliness to realize the importance of spiritual things! Forty minutes to break the spell of sin upon a multitude of hearts, and to induce them to prepare to meet their God! Forty minutes to get dull ears to listen to the Spirit's voice! Forty minutes to bring dead men to life! How awful that he should prostitute his oratory and opportunity to draw a crowd and win them to himself and not to Christ!

A preacher is not a great man, but he must preach great matters. Some men preach who appear to be as clerks in a poor store. They are very busy, but they have no goods.

A man has no right to ask the attendance and attention of a people unless he has something to say. Blessed is that pastor of whom his people say, "He always has something fresh for us from the Word of God."

Many could retire to their homes after some sermons and share the sentiments of Robert Louis Stevenson, who wrote in his journal these words, "Went to church today and was not greatly depressed." If our preaching leaves hearers in that state of mind, is it worth doing?

Gladstone charged the pulpiteers of his day with not being severe enough with their congregations. "They do not sufficiently lay hold upon the souls and consciences of their hearers their moral obligations, and probe their hearts, and bring up their whole life and action to the bar of conscience."

People want to have everything in them spoken to except their consciences. Or as someone said, "We like to lie to ourselves about ourselves." In whatever age men have preached the Word of God they have had to reckon with that reality. In the days of Amos and Isaiah it was recorded that men said, "Prophesy unto us smooth things," and that desire and demand is ever-recurring. The late Bishop Gore put it this way: "The disease of modern preaching is its search after popularity." The true preacher, however, lifts his voice above the popular clamor of men for smooth things and issues forth the precious contents of Scripture with a "Thus saith the Lord."

Preachers are needed who are masters of wielding the Sword of the Spirit. God had such a man in Nathan when David needed to face his sin. Oh, if our preachers had something like Nathan's skill, serpent-like wisdom, and evangelical instancy. Nathan's sword was within an inch of the King's conscience before David knew that Nathan even had a sword. One sudden thrust and the king was at Nathan's feet.

Preach earnestly then. Earnestness comes from the heart moved by the Holy Spirit. A minister may shout and scream until his voice fails him, may pace from side to side in the pulpit like a tiger in his cage, may stomp his feet and pound the Bible, saw the air and weary both himself and his audience with violent demonstrations, and yet be utterly wanting in true earnestness.

The most intense earnestness will very often subdue the spirit and tone and manner of the preacher, and so prevent all boisterousness of expression and behavior. True earnestness cannot be assumed or counterfeited. It must be the genuine outflowing of the soul. Spurgeon said, "He who beats the air and bawls and raves and stamps means nothing; and the more a man really means what he says, the less vulgar vehemence will there be."

To some men preaching is sailing on a puddle. To such men preaching is a childish performance. A big man at a trivial task is ridiculous.

Feed my sheep! Sheep are largely dependent upon their shepherds for the riches or poverty of their provisions. To bring the thought home to our hearts, we are accounted responsible by our very calling for the feeding of immortal souls. They look to us for spiritual food and satisfaction.

When men and women come to our spiritual table, with aching cravings and desires, they are to find such provision as shall send them away with the words of the Psalmist upon their lips, "He satisfieth the longing soul, and filleth the hungry soul with goodness."

The business of the prophet is to fill the pulpit, not the pews. Nowhere in the New Testament is the size of the crowd the criterion of good preaching. Our Lord sometimes preached His crowd away. It is not our business to make the message acceptable, but to make it available. We are not out to make men like it, but to see that they get it.

Ours is the sacred privilege and responsibility to draw back the veils, remove the barriers, and bring men face to face with God. Our hearers will graciously forgive our odd mannerisms, our suicide of speech, and the poorness of presentation, if through that message there comes some authentic touch of the Unseen, some deep subduing sense of the Eternal. When our preaching causes men to see Christ and impels the hearers to prayer, you may be sure, despite its shortcomings, it is preaching indeed.

3 CHARACTER AND CONDUCT

J. D. Jones said, "The one indispensable condition of our usefulness and success in the work of the ministry is that we be good men, men of pure and holy life, men of God. We may be good ministers without being either learned or eloquent, but we cannot be good ministers without being good men. The effect of our words will depend upon our lives, for it is always the man behind the speech who wields the power."

The preacher IS the sermon. No matter what his theory may be, his character, conduct, and personality preach to every beholder.

The pulpit may be the center of overwhelming power, and it may be the scene of tragic disaster. A church is not likely to rise above its pastor in spirituality and conduct. The old adage still holds, "Like priest, like people!"

Andrew Murray said, "The first duty of every clergyman is to beg of God, very humbly, that all he wants done in his hearers may first be fully and truly done in himself."

God makes a man; the man makes a ministry; the ministry makes a church. Phillip Brooks commented, "The pastor must be a preacher that he may keep the dignity of his work alive.

The preacher who is not a pastor grows remote. The pastor who is not a preacher grows petty."

Preacher, love your Lord, love your people, and love the lost. To love to preach is one thing; to love those to whom we preach is quite another. Unless a man be a good lover of people, he has positively no business in the ministry. If people try him, if he secretly despises a crowd, if he ever in his most trivial and private moments thinks folks cheap, and in his secret thought classifies them so, then he must forbear the ministry. We dare not call any man common or unclean. To love Christ and not love those to whom God has called us to minister is practical impossibility.

It is no trouble to preach, but a vast trouble to construct a preacher. When Gehazi went at Elisha's command to resurrect the dead, he took the prophet's staff with him; but no miracle happened, for the virtue of the staff was negated by the hands that held it. It could be that we become so busy preparing our sermons that we omit the preparation of ourselves. Keep thyself with all diligence!

The minister must not fail in the great matters of morality, honesty, and integrity. His private life must ever keep tune with his ministry, or his day will soon set, and the sooner he retires the better, for his continuance in his office will only dishonor the cause of God and ruin himself.

Be fit for your work, and you will never be out of it.

God prepares a man for what He is preparing him. Before God works THROUGH a man, He works IN a man, because the work that we do is the outgrowth of the life that we live. Little wonder that Alexander Whyte told a group of theological students, "A congregation is awaiting you, to be made by you, after you are made by God."

Whatever "call" a man may pretend to have, if he has not been called to holiness, he certainly has not been called to the ministry.

The pastor's priority is to live obediently before the Lord. Dr. Clarence Macartney wrote it well: "The better the man, the better the preacher. When he kneels by the bed of the dying or when he mounts the pulpit stairs, then every self-denial he has made, every Christian forbearance he has shown, every resistance to sin and temptation, will come back to him to strengthen his arm and give conviction to his voice. Likewise every evasion of duty, every indulgence of self, every compromise with evil, every unworthy thought, word, or deed, will be there at the head of the pulpit stairs to meet the minister on Sunday morning, to take the light from his eye, the power from his blow, the ring from his voice, and the joy from his heart."

4 PREACHING AND PRAYER

Put the Word of God in any man's hand, and set the Throne of Grace wide open before him, and you need no omniscience to tell you that man's true value. If he lets his Bible lie unopened and unread, if he lets God's Throne of Grace stand till death, idle and unwanted, if the depth and the height, the nobleness and the magnificence, the goodness and the beauty of divine things have no command over him, and no attraction to him, then you do not wish to know the meanness of that man's mind. Look at what he has chosen! Look and weep at what he has neglected and has for ever lost!

The man who is much in prayer instinctively finds God's garden, its fragrant spices and wonderfully bracing air, and he can lead others to it. Men never learn to pray in public; they learn in private. If we are never in Gethsemane when alone, we shall not find our way there with the crowd.

E. B. Earle, the famous Baptist evangelist, gave this observation, " I have noticed that as soon as the pastors have melted down and led the way the churches have usually quickly followed."

S. D. Gordon wrote, "The greatest thing anyone can do for God or man is to pray. It is not the only thing; but it is the chief thing. The great people of the earth are the people who pray."

Eternity will reveal that the greatest benefactors of the world are men of prayer. Sir Isaac Newton, the immortal scientist, said, "I can take my telescope and look millions and millions of miles into space, watch the blazing suns and rolling planets in the infinite depths of immensity; but I can lay it aside and go into my room, shut the door, get down upon my knees in earnest prayer, and see more of heaven and get closer to God than when assisted by all the telescopes and material agencies of earth."

Let the man of God bathe his sermons with the dew of heaven in answer to prayer, and there will be a thawing of cold hearts, a melting together of God and souls which is itself a revival. God will answer earnest prayer. Let him therefore who drives the chariot of the Lord not be frightened by the fire of the Holy Spirit.

Alexander Whyte said, "Our office is the 'Royal Priesthood.' God said, 'Ask me of things concerning my sons, and concerning the work of my hands command ye me.' What a thing for God to say to man! What a magnificent office! Hear Him! The King stretches forth His scepter. He has commanded your request!"

Let us pray then. God wants to share with us. He allows us to be the architects of our own estates and the fashioners of our own fortunes. The acceptableness and power of prayer are in direct proportion to the secrecy and the spirituality of it.

Lord, teach us to pray. Exercise imagination when praying. Napoleon once said that "men of imagination rule the world." They rule the pulpit also. Imagination, as God in His goodness gave it at first to man, is nothing less than the noblest intellectual attribute of the human mind. Yet the imagination is far more to the spiritually minded man than it is an intellectual attribute.

Never neglect imagination when praying. Never once shut your eyes and bow your knees to pray, without, at the same moment, opening the eyes of your imagination. Shut not your outward eyes and not at the same moment open the eyes of your inner man. Let your imagination sweep up through the whole visible heavens, up to the heaven of heavens. Let it sweep and soar on shining wing past sun, moon, stars. Let her leave Orion and Pleiades far behind. Let her heart swell and beat as she realizes God made all these things—the God you are approaching in prayer.

Praying, with the imagination all awake and all employed, will soon drink up your whole soul into itself. You will then be "praying always." You will have gotten your eyes as well as your hands on God.

Consider the heavens, the work of His fingers, the moon and the stars, which He hath ordained; consider the intellectual heavens also, angels and archangels, cherubim and seraphim; consider mankind also, made in the image of God; consider Jesus Christ, the express image of His person; consider a past eternity and a coming eternity, and the revelation thereof that is made to us in the Word of God and in the hearts of His people—and I defy you to think otherwise than magnificently of God. AND THEN, AFTER ALL THAT, I equally defy you to forget, or neglect, or restrain prayer. Once you begin to think aright of Him who is the Hearer of Prayer, and Who waits, in all His magnificence, to be gracious to you—I absolutely defy you to live any longer the life which you now live.

T. DeWitt Talmadge said, "Show me a man who prays, and his strength and power cannot be exaggerated. Why, just give to a man this power of prayer and you give him almost omnipotence!"

5 BURDEN AND BLESSING

Hercules is pictured as leaning, stooped, holding up the weight of the world. The crush of the preacher's load would break him to the earth except he has a "very present help."

Charles E. Jefferson said, "A shepherd cannot shine. He cannot cut a figure. His work must be done in obscurity. His work calls for continuous self-effacement. It is a form of service which eats up a man's life. It makes a man old before his time. Every shepherd lays down his life for his sheep."

The man who undertakes to induce a lot of hard-hearted, mature rams with stiff necks and stout horns, to sit down at the feet of Him who is the Way, the Truth, and the Life, and to stay there until they have learned their lessons, is soon to find he has a task not akin to recreation. The pastor might just as well realize at the start what he is in for. He will know burden in abundance.

The minister's work is never done. He does not punch a clock at eight in the morning and four in the afternoon. He cannot leave his burden at the factory. When a pastor identifies himself sympathetically with the needs of people, the time never comes when he is free. His church is with him in his down-sitting and his up-rising, and it goes with him in all his ways. If his thoughts ascend up into heaven, the saints of his flock are there needing to be made more saintly than they really are. If in some dark hour his heart makes its bed in hell, he may find some of his members there. Even the night is light about him, because the darkness never hides from the eyes of the faithful pastor the pleading faces of those who look to him for help.

The rest of the life of a pastor will always find him getting ready for next Sunday. No man in the active ministry ever escapes from that sense of responsibility. It is always there, like the power of gravitation. And there never was a sermon which could not have been made better by another hour or two of hard work.

If ever a man finds the work of the ministry becoming manageable and surmountable, an undemanding vocation without strain or any encumbering load of care, he is to be pitied, not congratulated: for he has so flagrantly lost touch with One whose ministry of reconciliation could be accomplished and fulfilled only through Gethsemane and Calvary.

The work of the ministry is very difficult. Ian Macpherson in his book, The Burden of the Lord, makes this observation, "No man who is not prepared to work himself to death has any right in the ministry at all. Where is there a more despicable creature than he who spares himself in the cause of Christ? And how can one who is habitually taking things easy convincingly preach the Gospel of the Cross? The thing just cannot be done."

Spurgeon's advice to his ministerial students was, "Kill yourselves with work, and then pray yourselves alive again."

Toil in the Lord's vineyard will take its toll on any dedicated person. Just three years in the ministry made an old man of our Lord. The Jews made rough guesses at his age. "Thou are not yet fifty years old" (Jn. 8:57). Fifty! He was only thirty! Days of toil and nights of prayer had taken their toll.

Is it any wonder that Paul breathed aloud the continual fear of his heart, "Woe is me if I preach not the Gospel." So great is the burden of the ministry and so great are the consequences of neglecting it, that there is an unceasing Gethsemane be-setting the heart and mind of one privileged to stand before men as the voice of God. We dare not let up, we dare not fail. Perhaps saintly Alexander Whyte best expressed that fearful feeling of accountability, when he spoke the tumult of the pastor's heart, "Oh, my brethren, the never-to-be-redeemed opportunities of our pulpits; and the lasting blame of God and our people, and of our consciences, for the misuse and neglect of our pulpits! Rock of Ages, cleft for ministers!"

No true-hearted man of God wants to settle for less than the smile of God upon his ministry. His burden is for that blessing. He seeks thus to love the Lord his God with all his heart and mind and soul and strength. What could be more condemning than the charge that our God made against the pastor of Ephesus? How dreadful to have Christ Himself say plainly to any minister that he had left his first love to his Lord and his work! And with that Voice, sounding as many waters, came this warning that unless he repented and returned and did again those first works, his candle would be removed out of its place and given to another. Surely this has been repeated through the years and many a man's work has been given to another.

6 SAINT AND SINNER

Paul, the greatest of preachers, said, "Christ Jesus came into the world to save sinners; of whom I am chief." He did not say that he "had been chief of sinners," but he knew himself to still be the chief of sinners.

The true preacher feels with Paul that he too is not only chief of the sinners, but least of all saints. It is like Alexander Whyte, who in his chapter on David and His Vices, in Bible Characters, says, "I am warned of God that with all my study and all my watchfulness and all my prayerfulness, the deceitfulness and internal hypocrisy of my own heart will still deceive me. Well, all I shall say in answer to that is this—that if my heart is worse than I know it to be, then the God of all grace, with all the blood of His Son, and with all the patience and power of His Spirit, help me."

Only once did God choose a completely sinless preacher. Always, but that once, God has chosen sinful men, and not seldom the most sinful of men to speak to their fellow men about salvation and sin. It takes a great sinner to preach, as well as to hear.

If you are calling and inspiring lepers with passion, that passion will come with a recognition of the leprosy of your own heart.

David was both Israel's greatest sinner and saint. David, though the Prodigal Son of the Old Testament, was still the anointed of the Lord, the King of Israel, the man after God's own heart.

A story is told of a farmer, who, after finishing his Saturday chores, put on his Sunday clothes and started off to see and hear saintly John Fletcher preach. (John Wesley said of Fletcher, "He was the holiest man I ever knew.") When the farmer passed a neighbor who was working, the neighbor stopped him and asked where he was going all dressed up. The farmer replied, "I am going to see Fletcher and hear him preach." On Monday morning he was returning and the same neighbor stopped him again, and asked if he had seen Mr. Fletcher. The farmer replied, "No, I saw no man save Jesus Christ and Him crucified."

The more true spirituality any man has, the more honed will be that man's sensibility to sin and to the exceeding sinfulness of sin. The holier men become in the sight and estimation of both God and men the more hideous and hopeless do they become to themselves.

Samuel Rutherford, perhaps the saintliest of them all, said, "When I look at my sinfulness, my salvation is to me my Saviour's greatest miracle." And the title page of John Bunyan's incomparable auto-biography says, "Grace abounding to John Bunyan, the chief of sinners. Come and hear, all ye that fear God, and I will declare what He hath done for my soul." Jacob Behmen said, "My heart is the very dunghill of the devil, and it is no easy work to wrestle with him on his own chosen ground. But wrestle with him on that ground I must, and that the whole of my life to the end."

It was Martin Luther who said, "When a man like me comes to know the plague of his own heart, he is not miserable only—he is absolute misery itself; he is not sinful only—he is absolute sin itself." And saintly Jonathan Edwards said, "It has often appeared to me that if God were to mark my heart-iniquity my bed would be in hell."

The holier and the more heavenly minded a minister is, the more he lays himself open to a life of unspeakable temptation. With every new step forward in spirituality, with every new revelation from the Word of God and of Himself, with every deeper entrance of the Spirit of God into his heart and conscience, a minister's temptations multiply upon him, till he feels himself to be the most beset of all men that dwell upon the earth.

God's men have walked humbly through the tumult of their times. Vilified of men, they have been declared the offscouring of a world unworthy of them. Strange as it seems, they agree with their accusers and moreover accuse themselves, pouring out upon their own hearts a loathsome load of contempt and condemnation at their own unworthiness and unfitness. John the Baptist felt his unworthiness as he walked through the wilderness pointing men to the Lamb of God. That loin-clad evangelist came with the sweet taste of honey in his mouth and the sound of divine authority in his voice, all the while confessing himself unworthy to even bow down to unloose the latchet of the shoes of his Lord.

The closer one is drawn to the blessed Saviour the more unworthy he realizes himself to be. Is it any wonder then that someone voiced this feeling of heart, saying, "If there is anything in which I would be inclined to contradict my Lord, it would be if I heard Him say, 'Well done, thou good and faithful servant.' "

7 WEAKNESS AND WANTS

O frail man, weak and wanting, who is sufficient for these things? This question has forced its way out of the heart of every servant of God amid the heat of battle. Paul himself asked the question long ago (II Cor. 2:16), and gave us a blessed insight when he added the words, "Not that we are sufficient of ourselves . . . but our sufficiency is of God" (II Cor. 3:5). His question comes forth like the cry of a spent warrior, but the answer which follows is like the shout of the victor. It is a contrast of moods. Paul was like us all. One moment he could be deep in the valley and the next moment high on the mountain; one moment absolutely fearless in the all-conquering power of God, and the next moment shaking like a reed in the wind at the very remembrance of his own weakness. He trembled when he thought of that. He feared no man except himself. The foes without never disturbed Paul; it was the foe within that did, that treacherous weakness of his own heart. When Paul placed his absolute insufficiency alongside of God's all-sufficiency, he revealed both his weakness and his wants.

Only that man is "sufficient for these things" who reckons on the resources of God. Hudson Taylor understood this and wrote, "All God's giants have been weak men, who did great things for God because they reckoned on His being with them." He concluded that "Want of trust is at the root of almost all of our sins and weaknesses."

J. H. Jowett was one of those great men always conscious of his weaknesses and shortcomings. One time when he was to speak at Northfield, one of the brethren gave an opening prayer with this inspired supplication: "O Lord, we thank Thee for our brother. Now BLOT HIM OUT! Reveal Thy glory to us in such blazing spendor that he shall be forgotten." Jowett thought the request was absolutely appropriate and trusted the prayer was answered.

It was Paul who said, "Neither is he that planteth any thing, neither he that watereth." Take it by faith, we are nothing! This is especially true of the man who thinks he can preach. Like the man who had an intense desire to preach, and pressed for opportunities until he was given permission to deliver a trial sermon. Upon announcing his text he found himself bereft of every idea but one, which he uttered feelingly as he came down. "My brethren, if any of you think it is an easy thing to preach, I advise you to come up here and have all the conceit taken out of you."

We have the treasure of the gospel in earthen vessels, and if there be a flaw in the vessel here and there let none wonder. Had it not been for the weakness of the broken wing some might have lost themselves in the clouds.

Who can help being weak and weary and out of breath when the race set before us is continued without intermission.

Despite the fact that the vessel is of clay, and the humanness of the man of God is revealed in weakness, yet the preacher holds a kind of vicarious and representative position before both heaven and hell, and the swordsmen and archers of both realms seem to make him their target. Who then can judge the severity of the embattled life of the man of God who has both heaven and hell setting on him continually?

It was Alexander Whyte who wrote, "Oh poor and much-to-be-pitied minister! With Satan concentrating all his fiery darts upon you, with the deep-sunken pillars of his seat not yet dug out of your hearts, with all his captains fighting day and night for the remnants of their master's power within you, and all the time, a far greater than Satan running you through and through with that terrible sword of His till there is not a sound spot in you—Oh, most forlorn and afflicted of men! Oh, most bruised in your mind, and most broken in your heart, of all men! Pity your ministers, my brethren, and put up with much that you cannot yet understand or sympathize with in them. And never for a day forget to pray for them."

8 DISCOURAGEMENT AND DEPRESSION

Charles Haddon Spurgeon said, "I am the subject of depressions of spirit so fearful that I hope none of you ever get to such extremes of wretchedness as I go to." Perhaps one reason Spurgeon was able to bring such great comfort to his hearers was that he knew the problem of depression first hand.

It seems that depression and discouragement are occupational hazards, if not occupational diseases of the ministry. John Donne called them "The damp of hell," and surely they are.

Even Elijah was sure he had failed. Under the Juniper Tree he said, "I am not better than my fathers!" When a pastor decides he has failed, Satan has found an opening in his armour, and you can be sure that enemy will take advantage of it. Francois Fenelon said, "Discouragement serves no possible purpose; it is simply the despair of wounded self-love."

Martin Luther's two suggestions for overcoming despair were: "Exercise faith in Christ, and get downright angry!"

Pilgrim's Progress leaves us this encouragement: "Be of good cheer my brother, for I feel the bottom, and it is good."

It is when a man strikes rock-bottom in his sense of nothingness that he suddenly finds he has struck the Rock of Ages.

Samuel Rutherford used to say that whenever he found himself in the cellars he began to busy himself looking for the King's wine.

In the final analysis, discouragement is a spiritual problem and can only be fought with spiritual weapons. Pray then and be of good cheer; the lowest ebb can be the turn of the tide!

It has been said "The preacher is always on the brink of the abyss!" Doubtless the words were meant to convey that preaching which sways the preacher's emotions, moving him like a gale upon the sea, making great demands upon his nerves, and often producing physical and emotional exhaustion, may also make him the victim of deep depression and nervous impoverishment, causing his moral defenses to be relaxed and allowing the enemy to leap within the gates and imprison his spirit in carnal bondage.

A discouraged pastor sought the counsel of Alexander Whyte and was given this advice: "Never think of giving up preaching! The angels around the throne envy your great work. Discouragement can rob us of our vitality and vision. How vast the importance of keeping our spirituality honed well." Charles E. Jefferson said, "Self-preparation is the most difficult work a preacher has to do. A preacher who is spiritually anemic, or intellectually impoverished, or morally depleted, will wish often for a juniper tree."

Is it to be wondered at that many a man of God, like Elijah and Jeremiah, has tried to run away from a commission so crushing and intolerable? Nothing but the grace of God can hold him to it. The magnitude of that commission is overwhelming and the first element in humility.

Every man of God has had those discouraging moments when he was ready to resign, and knew all the time that he could not. Jeremiah had a time like that (Jer. 20:9). That broken-hearted prophet announced the impossible: he resigned and then declared immediately that he could not resign; he quit but he could not quit. Any true man of God can understand the crisis that Jeremiah had.

Jeremiah said, "Oh that I had in the wilderness a lodging place of wayfaring men" (9:2). He is not the first preacher who wanted to quit and go into the motel business. Many have thought that testifying to tourists might accomplish more than taking the tribulations of the pastorate. But the most miserable of men are ministers who have quit. Some do their own resigning while others are spared the trouble. Some spend years resigning while others leave overnight with the parting word "Nevermore!" The faithful preacher has no bed of roses, but for a God-called man to become anything else is to rest his soul on a bed of thorns.

There is not a man who has labored in the service of God but who will say "Amen" to the fact that Christian work is both the most discouraging and the most encouraging work in the world. Let him who sets out to toil in the vineyard of the Lord get ready for both troubles and triumphs, and may the Lord help him not to be upset by either. Some days he will find himself crawling and some days he will find himself flying, and it is hard to say which places him in the greater danger.

Discouragement comes to all. Those who have read the treasures of Matthew Henry's Commentary know that he wrote, in his last days, concerning his pastorate: "Though the people at Chester are a most loving people, and many of them have had and have an exeeding value for me and my ministry; yet I have not been without my discouragements there, and those such as have tempted me to think my work in that place has been in a great measure done. Many that have been catechized with us and many that have been long communicants with us have left us and very few have been added to us."

God plants His wheat where it may produce the best yield. He places his own men where He chooses to fulfill a purpose. Never forget that John was on Patmos for ". . . the Word of God, and . . . the testimony of Jesus Christ . . ." (Rev. 1:2). Patmos was not a promotion to a larger congregation, but it provided for us the Revelation. John didn't resign, he stayed on and saw it through to the glorious end.

9 PERILS AND PRIVILEGES

Perils are ever the attendants of privilege, and they are thickest around the most exalted stations. It is perhaps life's saddest and most pathetic tragedy, the spectacle of a man, who having "preached to others" should himself "become a castaway."

Perhaps no others are able to conceive the insidious and deadly perils which infest the life of a man of God. The measure of our privilege is just the measure of our dangers. The inventory of our garden would also give an inventory of the destructive forces that haunt every flower and shrub and tree. It is literally and awfully true that "where grace abounds," sin may also abound.

Perils have a common and fatal tendency to snare us away from God. They will lead the preacher away from the "snows of Lebanon," from the great gathering ground of spiritual resources, where the mighty rivers rise and flow on to a strong and efficient ministry. There is no sight on earth more pathetic than a preacher of the Gospel who has by the wiles and guiles of this world been separated from God.

One of the gravest perils which beset the ministry of this country is a restless scattering of energies over an amazing multiplicity of interests, which leaves no margin of time or strength for receptive and absorbing communion with God.

Preachers might well consider the words of Lord Bryce given to Viscount Grey when he confessed to him the difficulty he experienced in composing long speeches. Bryce said, "You need not be disturbed as long as you feel like that. The time to be alarmed is when you find that you can speak quite easily without having anything to say." Coleridge shrewdly described it as a "premature and unnatural dexterity in the combination of words." Let that man beware who is gifted with the facility of utterance.

For the lack of carefulness and prayerfulness and discretion men of God have fallen from the summits of fame and usefulness to the depths of sin and disgrace, from which they could never rise. Some have had to be put out of the ministry. Churches have been divided, the cause of righteousness so dishonored that it would take the united labors of a generation of godly men to erase the stains!

Next to insincerity nothing so discounts one's ministry as indolence. Many preachers have been snared by this peril. Many ministers do nothing more than draw their salary and breath.

There are many ministers of rare promise whose gristle never turns to bone. When the devil sees a man marching through difficulties and mounting the heights of success with the mailed limbs of a giant, he lays a snare for his advancing feet. It may be pride of intellect. It may be bodily self-indulgence. It may be compromise. He who is captured and falls may be restored again by the mercy of God. But the enemy of all good never forgets to use it to cripple his usefulness. Henceforth he walks under a shadow. There is an interrogation mark after his name. He may never fully recover.

Paul knew that a preacher's first commodity was himself. He knew how easily the pearl of personality could be lost, how easily one could disqualify himself in the race. To keep yourself is worth battling for. A reputation once broken may possibly be repaired, but the world will always keep their eyes on the spot where the crack was.

The most godly of men can be sidetracked by the peril of familarity. Nothing can be more devastating to a deep Christian experience than being in the midst of religious activity all the time. It can usher one gradually into spiritual stupefaction. The result is professionalism. One may be busy with the things of God and all the while be getting further away from experiencing the reality of the very truths he labors to perpetuate. Robertson of Bright was right when he spoke of "the hardening influences of spiritual things."

That hundreds have missed their way and stumbled against a pulpit is sorrowfully evident from the fruitless ministries and decaying churches which surround us. It is a fearful calamity to a man to miss his calling, and to the church upon which he imposes himself.

Privileges carry their own perils. Perhaps the peril of Solomon lay in the privileges his position afforded. Solomon's wisdom and knowledge were comprehensive. He was a master of moral and spiritual truth. He knew the claims of God. He knew the power of temptation. He knew the power of women and the power of wine. He knew the weakness of the human heart. He knew the consequences of sin, yet he determined to risk them. Thus Solomon in his fall belied himself. He tore down in his after life, what he built up in his former life. He stood at last the living contradiction to his earlier profession. Sad that a man should so reverse himself, should so neutralize his own record, should so undo, with one hand, what he had done with the other.

A man's fall eclipses all the good he has accomplished. That is a solemn thought. A minister may preach for forty years like an angel, and then, by one flagrant sin or by one treason to truth make it so that men do not care to hear him preach and blush to speak his name. Solomon was buried in silence. He filled a large space but proved unworthy of it, and departed leaving only the shadow of remembrance.

10 MAN AND MESSAGE

We preach Christ! What a preacher Paul was. He moved amid the garishness of Ephesus, and Corinth, and Rome, but he never borrowed the artificial splendor of his surroundings and thereby eclipsed the Cross. No "way of the world" seduced him from that blessed theme. Wherever he went, whether to a little prayer meeting by the river side in Philippi, or amid the intellectuals of Athens, he "determined to know nothing among men save Jesus Christ and Him crucified."

Beware of losing sweetness and love and grace in your preaching. Because of agitated conditions in the church, frequently brought on by themselves, some pastors have used the sacred pulpit for denunciatory and merciless preaching. They boast of their uncompromising stand, and "skin" and "peel" and "hang the hides from the fence," and refuse to take anyone's advice. A preacher who does not carry with him the mantle of charity has missed his calling, or unfitted himself to discharge his duties.

Never allow yourself to lack that fine fragrance which makes people know that you dwell in "the King's gardens." That was true of Onesiphorus. Paul wrote an exquisite line portraying his friend and also describing this very characteristic pastoral service, "He oft refreshed me." He carried the heavenly atmosphere with him.

Uncle Bud Robinson testified to his being a man of God. He was once a worker in a camp meeting with Dr. Henry C. Morrison when an interesting incident occured. One Sunday morning during the love feast Uncle Bud got up to testify about his wonderful Lord and got so stirred and blessed that he fell under the mighty power of God. The crowds gathered around but Dr. Morrison told them to stand back and give Robinson room. He said, "The dear fellow has just broken off more than he can chew."

ANY HILL CAN MAKE AN ECHO. "I am the voice of ONE," said John. Can you say that, preacher? Or must you, in all fidelity to truth say, "I am an echo." If a man is but an echo he is common-place, for echoes multiply. But if he be a voice—men will stop, listen, and marvel.

The pulpit is not a sounding board. It is a voice from heaven. It is the God-invasion of this world. Therefore we must be a voice and not an echo. On any given day visitors might well ask of some pulpits, "Who preaches here?" A just reply might be, "Most anybody preaches here, but Brother Ditto is the mouthpiece." How sweet it would be if the question at our churches was, "Who preaches here?" and the answer would be," Christ preaches here; our pastor is His voice."

We have the wilderness; God give us a voice!

When Hudson Taylor was being introduced to a congregation as their guest speaker he was referred to as "our illustrious guest." Taylor rose and began his sermon saying, "I am the little servant of an illustrious Master."

Spurgeon used to implore his students to "preach nothing down but the devil, and nothing up but Christ."

Anything savoring of unreality in the pulpit is doubly offensive. Perhaps there is nothing more deadly and more infallibly destructive to the atmosphere of reality in preaching than the "pulpit voice", the "ministerial whine." How much better it is if men hear us, as they did John, and know it to be "the voice of One." It is a different kind of preaching which creates that heavenly hush which tells that Christ is in the midst, that leaves men with the knowledge that they have both seen and heard reality.

The world counts as safe, as sound, as judicious, the quiet, respectable preacher of form; the quiet, respectable preacher of philosophy; the polished man who flatters the flesh and saves it; and counts the downright, the earnest man as crazy. Should there be any evidences of the Holy Spirit's power in such a man's message, the world cries out that he is "beside himself," unhinged, delirious, full of new wine, a madman.

Such things have been said of men in our day. Such things were said of D. L. Moody and Charles Haddon Spurgeon. Spurgeon was called a charlatan, sensational, and was caricatured and held up to ridicule in every way. Of Spurgeon, George Sayles Bishop wrote, "Whoever saw that Elijah-like man of God move slowly, heavily into the pulpit, whoever felt the awful hush on the assembled thousands as he rose up to pray, whoever found himself brought, as there, face to face with the vast, unveiling eternity, must have known in his heart the sheer impossibility of such falsehoods; must have had the profoundest conviction that, whatever might be the most startling, vehement, even supernatural flights of his terrible earnestness, never could such a man be anything else than a man, prostrated in soul, overawed, overwhelmed and laboring under the pressure, solemnity, and power of the Spirit of God."

Earnestness! Would to God that we were more earnest! Power lies, for the most part, in earnestness. Other elements which enter into power are nothing without earnestness. Earnestness is power in action, the white heat of power. Can we be too earnest? Measured against the hell into which sinners are staggering, and the heaven into which new converts are sweeping, can an honest man, moved by God, be too earnest? Put in contrast with eternal interests, eternal magnitudes, was ever any man too earnest in preaching the Word of God?

11 THE SPIRIT AND SUCCESS

The greatest quest in the life of a servant of God is the fellowship of the Spirit. It is the "manna from heaven" for his feasting, the "water of life" for his thirsting, the "oil of gladness" for his preaching. To lose that communion is tragedy; to forsake it is apostasy; to regain it is ecstasy; to preserve it is priority.

The blessed Holy Spirit has been given to glorify Christ. When Henry Ward Beecher began his ministry, he was baffled by a disappointing absence of results and an almost total lack of response. The chariot wheels dragged; there were no visible signs of an awakening; the indifferent remained sunk in their indifference. But one day the thought gripped him; "There was a reason why, when the apostles preached, they succeeded, and I will find it out if it is to be found out." He discovered the reason was the preaching of Christ, and the results and success in his ministry were immediate.

The Holy Spirit is absolutely essential to the minister and the effectiveness of his ministry. Without Him that office is mere trivia. Unless the preacher has the Spirit of the prophets resting upon him, the mantle he wears is nothing more than a garment of deception. If the Spirit of God does not rest upon us and our ministry we are as sounding brass and tinkling cymbals; having a form but not the fire.

Oh, for the touch and wisdom of the Spirit of God. It is He who will give our hands the skill of a surgeon to rightly divide the Word. It is He who will grant us wisdom to use the sacred balances in weighing out the proper portions of manna for the needs of our people. It is He who will season our speech with grace that His Word be made more beautiful and our Lord more glorified. It is He who will press the live coal from the altar to our lips and open our mouths that we may show forth the praises of the Lord, or else we shall not speak with power.

It is the Spirit of God who is our Helper and Comforter. At times we may be crushed to the earth in depression, or carried to the skies on wings of delight. At one and the same time we may find ourselves groaning for the souls of lost men, or mourning over the lack of growth in grace in some members of our flock. We may be preaching and look into certain faces and say, "The dew is descending here," and then look into other faces and perceive they are as dewless as Gilboa's mountain. But the dews of Heaven must fall, for we must have such seals of grace upon our ministry; and who can bestow such grace and grant such help but the Spirit of God.

The fact that there are so many fruitless ministries testifies to the lack of recognizing the person and power of the Holy Spirit. The words of Robert Hall are as forceful now as when he poured them forth like molten lava: "The most eminent and successful preachers of the gospel . . . a Brainerd, a Baxter, and a Schwartz, have been the most conspicuous for simple dependence on spiritual aid; and no success whatever has attended the ministrations of those by whom this doctrine has either been neglected or denied."

It is imperative that the Holy Spirit attend our preaching with His witness. Charles G. Finney, called the prince of evangelists of all time, said, "No human eloquence can ever convert a soul unless the Spirit of God sends the truth home and makes it effectual."

How horrifying the thought a man might so neglect or deny the Holy Spirit that He would withdraw Himself from that man and his ministry and the words "Ichabod" be written for all to see. True, we know the Spirit of God never leaves nor forsakes the man who is born of Him, but that does not guarantee that He may not remove the halo of blessing from that man's service. If such things as prayerlessness, impurity, pride, etc., disqualify the ordinary believer from enjoying communion with God, then surely those same things can disqualify the preacher from experiencing the power of God. Tremble and know that we may do despite to the Spirit of Grace and so insult and grieve Him that He will no more speak by us.

How fearful we should be that we not grieve the Holy Spirit. Let us tread softly before Him lest our ministry become bereft of blessing or come to sudden end. We might go on preaching and be like Samson supposing the Spirit of God to be upon us; neither suspecting ourselves nor suspected of others as being destitute of His power. It could be we might be smitten down in our prime, as were Nadab and Abihu, no more to be seen ministering before the Lord. Or we could be removed in the more golden years, like Hophni and Phineas, no longer to serve in the tabernacle of the congregation. We might try to labor on with a professional Phariseeism, presenting strange fire on the altar until the Lord will endure it no more. How terrible the thought! God may allow some to finish their work, but like Samson, the days be marred by blindness to blessing. The lap of Delilah and the camp of Dan are not conducive to greater power. Moses closed out his life work also, but under a cloud. His sin was not the startling scarlet one such as David's, nor the failure of a fearful Peter; his seemed an infinitesimal offence. God might have overlooked it in another, but not in Moses. He was a leader of God's people, a representative of Heaven.

If Moses be removed from office because He spoke unadvisedly with his lips, and if such a glorious servant as Paul feared becoming a castaway (disapproved) of God, then where do we stand? How dare we then lift our heads and imagine we are not expendable; that God would deal differently with us! For God to overlook sin in His servants would constitute a deception upon His people, and a disgrace to the office. Oh how fearful to be loved of God and called to stand before men in His stead. Who is faultless? Woe is me! Let us bow low and tremble before Him. The Lord our God is a jealous God, and it is a fearful thing to fall into the hands of the living God.

12 POLLEN AND PREACHING

The preacher's mind and heart and energy need pollen no less than the corn. He cannot work for it. It comes like the spring. Not all sermons are laid up like a brick wall. For so much sweat of brain one cannot count on so much crop of thought. Some sermons come only after the preacher has walked the rugged shorelines of this world and dipped his oars into its troubled waters. The wisdom of the man of God is to go where the Spirit of God may pollenate his brain and heart and energy.

It would shame God to have a lazy preacher in His vineyard, tarnishing with his touch the frost of the purple grape clusters. Preaching is far past work, it is inspirational, and pollen is needed. Preaching is a wafting of the wind of God, blowing of heavenly zephyrs across the star-strewn spaces, the blowing strangely sweet and quickening along the prairie lands of the soul.

The preacher is on an endless pilgrimage for pollen. He dare not always remain in the seclusion of his study. He must be out where the winds blow on the soul. He traverses a landscape of eternity in time, which is thought-haunted, and perhaps many an otherwise miserable message has been redeemed because of the immortalities that have crossed the preacher's path while he walked this solitary way. He finds the sweet nectar of God's

Word for his heart while he beholds the spiritual need of the world before his eyes. A man will serve his people far better who takes time to sit where they sit and walk where they walk, because he comes back bearing with him that precious pollen that will only provide his preaching greater yield.

Pollen begets the harvest. Of Henry Ward Beecher it was said that, when his mind was as empty as a haymow in spring, he would go to the Brooklyn Ferry and ride to and fro looking into the faces of the passengers, and out upon the river crowded with sea-going vessels. He was out where the pollen might be blowing.

13 BOOKS AND BUSYNESS

Paul said, "Bring the books." The pastor is a lover of books. Books are the juices squeezed from the cluster of the ages.

Any man engaged in any activity should be familiar with what others in his business have thought and said and done. The musician owes it to himself to know what his conferees have done. What the masters have wrought is of consequence to a craftsman. What a witless painter it would be who would not look at the canvas a mighty man had touched into immortality. Yet not more witless he than the preacher who does not familiarize himself with the sermons the mighty men of his calling have written or preached.

Read the works of others. The preacher lights his torch at all their fires, and then has a torch lit by the sun, which sun is Christ. With all that we have at our disposal, how great is the sin of being uninteresting. Compare the history of Athens or Rome with the history recorded from Genesis to Revelation, and those thrilling boasts of human grandeur and success become desolate and insipid before the marching on of God's Truth.

The man who continually reads or quotes the works of others has been said to creep along the shore of authors, as if he were afraid to thrust himself to the free compass of reasoning. In defense we might ask whether honey is the worse for being gathered from many flowers.

Make a sacrifice somewhere, but get books; and make sure you get good ones. A carpenter never has enough tools.

Let not books rule out the Book. Dr. Bonar of Scotland made this note in his journal: "By the grace of God and the strength of His Holy Spirit, I desire to lay down the rule not to speak to man until I have spoken to God: not to do anything with my hand until I have been upon my knees: not to read letters or papers until I have read something of the Holy Scriptures."

We are not always doing the most when we seem most busy. A busy man is rarely tempted. His thoughts are preoccupied, his life is full, he has no time to waste in dreams and dissipation.

Richard Baxter put it plainly to the clergy of his day, that "many a tailor goes in rags, that maketh costly clothes for others; and many a cook scarcely licks his fingers, when he hath prepared for others the most dainty dishes."

Beware the professional busy-ness which is but slackness in disguise.

Busy people often are fussy people. They lack the needed calm. John Wesley said, "I am always in haste, but never in a hurry."

Paul exhorted Timothy to "give attention to reading." Never be so busy that you are robbed of the time to read good books.

Dr. W. A. Criswell said that if he had but one thing to tell a young preacher it would be, "Keep the morning for God. Shut out the whole world and shut yourself to the Lord with a Bible in hand and with knees bowed in the presence of the holiness of the great Almighty."

The results will be that the people will praise God for the pastor who will spend time with an open Bible on his knees before the Judge of all the earth. It may seem strange, but any congregation would rejoice to think that their pastor came before them out of the Holy of Holies where he had met with the Lord face to face.

It was Theodore L. Cuyler who said, "Study your Bible and other good books in the morning, and the door plates of your people in the afternoon."

May we never be so busy with books that we lose sight of the souls of men. The man who is called to the ministry must never let his passion for souls die within him. That would mean a surrender of his God-given credentials, and the end of his effectiveness as a minister. Nothing that does not itself burn can kindle a flame in anything else. The fire must be in the heart of the preacher before there can be a tongue of fire in the pulpit or a flame kindled in the heart of any hearer.

The supposition that a man is so important he cannot afford time to make pastoral calls is a piece of irreligious conceit which is intolerable in a man who is to be servant of all. The greatest of mortal preachers, Paul, visited from house to house and did so betimes with tears.

14 COMMITMENT AND COMPROMISE

When Dr. Wilbur Chapman asked old General William Booth what was the secret of his great Christian success, he answered, "God has owned every inch of me."

Bishop Hendrix said, "The man who is always singing, 'Oh to be nothing, nothing,' has had his prayer answered, and his pound has been taken from him long ago. The healthy soul wants to be SOMETHING, for the glory of God, and has a purpose to that end from which he will never swerve."

Before we are fit for the highest and best service, the molten metal of our natures must be run into God's mold. No man is a chosen vessel unto God until he has surrendered his will to God. It is this obedience that makes a man a minister of God, and is the secret of his power with others.

Doddridge, the Bible commentator, wrote, "This day do I, with the utmost solemnity, surrender myself to Thee. I renounce all former lords that have had dominion over me: and I consecrate to Thee all that I am, and all that I have, the faculties of my mind, the members of my body, my worldly possessions, my time and my influence over others: to be all used according to Thy glory, as long as Thou continuest me in life: ever holding myelf in attentive posture to observe the first intimations of Thy will, and ready to spring forward with zeal and joy to the immediate execution of it. To Thee I resign myself and the management of all events pertaining to me and say without reserve, not my will but Thine be done."

W. E. Sangster said, "Lord, we don't mind who is second so long as Thou art first!"

We have a multitude of preachers now so distressingly smart that they do not believe much of anything, and are not certain of that. Let the man of God be weak and uncertain and hesitating, and the church is no longer a positive force.

Stick to the Book! Joseph Parker of the London Temple was a pillar of orthodoxy. In speaking of young preachers ruined by running after "new theories" he said, "I have seen enough dead theories and discarded hypotheses to fill a good sized cemetery. They entered the world like an amateur military band and coughed their way out of it like a squad of consumptive tramps!"

What shall it profit a man if he pack his church and let his whole audience go to hell?

Let it ever be borne in mind that the ministry is no little work, and can never be the work of a man with a divided heart. Once and for all he must abandon himself to the work of the Lord and to his Lord, and having put his hand to the plow, must not look back if he would succeed. He must love his Lord and love His work and stick to it through difficulties and discouragements, and not be given to change, for there is no discharge in this war.

The root of the whole matter is this: "It is not by might nor by power, but by my Spirit, saith the Lord of Hosts." It is He

Who converts from sin and renews the heart. He endues with power. The men in all ages who have been signally owned of God in the conversion of man, have been men much alone with God, men fired with one aim, consumed with one purpose; men aware of the constraining power of God, full of faith and the Holy Spirit.

Eagles are committed to the skies. Eagles are not found in swamps, nor do they fly in flocks. What we need today are more preachers who are committed to the Truth and a contradiction to the times. He may feel that such a life makes him a lone dissenter, a voice in the wilderness. It is not the business of the preacher to harmonize with the times. He is a soloist; he was never meant to play the accompaniment to anything. He will stand his ground and refuse to be swept off his feet by pernicious men or popular movements. Joseph Parker said, "There are those today who would clap their hands at the name of Bunyan who would not admit a living Bunyan into their fellowship." Organized religion hates the preacher whose headquarters is Heaven, whose Superintendent is God. The man of God must remember that prophets are needed, but not wanted.

15 ENTERTAINMENT AND EXHORTATION

While all about him swirl the currents of controversy, and the tide of trends, the man of God must stand like the undaunted rock of ages and sound forth the claims of the changeless Word of God. He stands an uncompromising bulwark amid the raging river of religious flotsam that seeks to dislodge him from his position. He is God's voice calling a prodigal people to return to the old paths, and the maintaining of historic Biblical landmarks. With great heaviness of heart, and often believing himself to be the lone dissenter, he seeks to reverse a generation bent on amusement to bow in amazement.

The man of God does not lose sight of the fact that the church once lived in the norm of amazement, "they were ALL amazed" (Acts 2:7); though now it is mired in amusement. He does not forget that the church was once held spellbound by amazement while worshipping in the presence of the thrice-holy God; though now a generation bred on entertainment sits waiting to be amused.

He does not forget that once sweet strains of Gospel music wooed men to God, and once old time preaching filled the altars with weeping mourners, while amazed onlookers cried, "What meaneth this?" He is beset with the burden of a church in show business, knowing that what was once an experience has become a performance.

It is thus a decadent generation that is being ministered to. A generation that cannot endure sound doctrine. A generation that chooses entertainment over exhortation. In characteristic unfamiliarity with the Word of God the voices of modern day prophets lead to the towering Babel of confusion by urging us to "get with it," to change our thinking and methods or get trampled under in the spiritual advance of the age. They cannot believe that the idea of spiritual entertainment is nowhere to be found in the Scriptures! They cannot believe that nothing was further from the minds of the early saints than the idea of entertaining, or "making it interesting." Beyond doubt the early church attracted multitudes, but it was the mighty power of God that drew the amazed throngs to ask, "What meaneth this?

The erosion of both music and message throughout christendom is embarrassingly evident. Self-styled servants of God blast forth with a deafening instrumental and vocal tumult that can only be accurately recorded by a seismograph. All spiritual message is aborted as the performers take their cue from Hollywood and jive for Jesus. Shades of Pentecost!

The church which once made its way into the jungle has now had the jungle make its way into the church. Music which once made folks pat their foot on the floor, now, for the most part, makes them bang their heads against the wall. Such degeneration has ushered us into the era where the crowd will stand and cheer and whistle and clamor for more such spiritual uplift. Yet when the pure preaching of God's Word is sounded forth so men can understand it, there is never heard an encouraging "Amen," nor does the crowd rise to cry for the Man of God to go on and give more edification. Of course, with Ananias and Sapphira on the official church boards, what more can be expected!

The preacher's task is akin to re-creation. He must be interesting without becoming an entertainer. He must captivate the minds of a spiritually shallow audience who crave religious entertainment, who have a love for the novel and the celebrated, who want to have their fantasy fed and their ears tickled, who will go for miles just to find from a speaker how many hairs are in the tail of the pale horse in Revelation. He discovers that a great many people are more interested in antichrist than they are in Christ!

While there is no command in the Word of God to entertain one another, there is a command to exhort one another. Amazement must take the place of amusement. Men must first ask in wonder, "What meaneth this?" before they will inquire, "What must we do?"

16 THE WONDER AND THE WORD

The pastor has to do with the Word of God at every point of his ministry. He must come to it in everything he undertakes. He is nothing without it. It is more to him than any—than all—other books. In the words of Thomas Murphy, "The Bible contains his credentials as an ambassador of Jesus Christ. It is the message which he is appointed to reiterate with all fervor to his fellow men. It is the treasury from which he can ever draw the riches of divine truth. It is the Urim and Thummin to which he has constant access to learn the mind of God with all clearness. It is the audience chamber where he will be received into the presence of the Lord and hear heavenly words. It is the armory from which he can be clothed with the panoply of salvation. It is the sword of the Spirit before which no enemy can possibly stand. It is his book of instructions wherein the great duties of his office are clearly defined. It is his mine of sacred wealth, the abundance of which he can never exhaust. The deeper he goes, the richer and more unbounded will its treasures appear."

Preach the Word of God! Spurgeon was a man of the Book. He was not limited to some formal exercise on a barren asphalt area, or confined to the limits of some small backyard. Hear him on the great themes of the Bible, and you have a sense of the vastness kindred to that which awes you when you listen to the Apostle Paul. Every apparently simple division in his sermon was like the turning of the telescope to some new galaxy of luminous wonders in the unfathomable sky.

It was said of the Bible preaching of Thomas Binney that "He seemed to look at the horizon rather than at an enclosed field, or a local landscape. He had a marvelous way of connecting every subject with eternity past and with eternity to come."

The effective preacher is the one who knows how to handle the "Sword of the Spirit" in the plainest, most direct and telling way. But when that sword is wrapped or sheathed in learned phrases, rhetorical embellishments, or philosophical refinements and speculations, its power of execution is vastly lessened, or entirely destroyed.

In an address given at the University of Edinburgh, in 1866, Thomas Carlyle remarked, "Can there be a more horrible object in existence than an eloquent man not speaking the Truth?"

Many men of the present day have eloquence, but the swords they flail are dull from fencing with issues. Surely a man needs to declare himself and take his stand, but none have a right in preaching to waste time on irrelevances. If we are not determined that in every sermon Christ is to be preached, it were better that we resign our commission forthwith and seek another vocation. Alexander Whyte, describing his Saturday walks with Marcus Dods, said, "Whatever we started off our conversation with, we soon made across country, somehow, to Jesus of Nazareth, to His death, and His resurrection, and His indwelling." And unless our sermons make for the same goal, and arrive at the same mark, our eloquence is for naught, they are simply an exercise in futility.

Oh, the awesome magnitude and magnificence of God's Word. We feel like David Livingstone who looked with wonder upon a dark continent, and said, "Oh, the vast unexplored regions of Africa! It will require centuries to penetrate its interior!"

Preacher, think then with wonder on the great continent of Scripture and move on into the vast unexplored regions of the Word of God! It will require the time of unending ages to penetrate its interior. There it is, a great unknown continent with a boundless interior awaiting our discovery, and we have but entered its borders. What a Book! It may be we shall follow the trails that have been opened, and perhaps strike an old footpath now and then which has been deserted, and it may be as the Holy Spirit guides that we shall find a trail or two where none have ever trod. There may be a great river of truth awaiting our discovery, or a transparent mirror-like lake of divine revelation, which no one ever knew was hidden in the vast distances of the hitherto hidden secrets of this Christ-revealing Book. There may be a snow-capped, sun-kissed mountain resplendent with redemptive glory arising in colossal magnitude before our gaze. The heart of this continent of countless conquests calls the man of God onward.

Lord, grant us journeying mercies!

17 HELPMATE AND HOME

Nothing is more supremely important, after his personal salvation, than the preacher's choice of his life companion.

To find the fitting helpmate he must watch and pray. When the ministerial student was seeking advice on finding a wife, the wise old professor suggested that he "pray with one eye open!"

The death knell of many an otherwise successful ministry is rung at the marriage altar.

Of all the sad experiences in a pastor's life, what can be more truly pathetic than for a really gifted, godly and much loved pastor, to be driven out of one pastorate after another by the razor-edged, untamed tongue of a hot-tempered, indiscreet wife; or to be driven from the ministry altogether by her continual restlessness and resentment with her lot and life.

No other man more truly needs a wife than a preacher. She is his protection from temptation and censure, his teacher about the family relations, his friendly and most helpful advisor, his most kindly and charitable critic, and his other self. Her value is beyond estimation, and some have come to the realization that the wife God has given him is no less than angel disguised in womanhood.

God Himself was hard put to describe a virtuous woman. He simply summed it up in "a good THING"; adding that her price is far above rubies. She becomes the gems on the crown of a man's ministry. Though she often deserves more credit than her husband, she seldom receives it. No life is more lonely, more unrecognized, more trying, than that of the pastor's wife. Her life, her home, her husband, her time, are really never quite her own.

It isn't long after a woman marries before she suddenly realizes that she did not marry a man, she married a MINISTER! Between the two there is a great gulf fixed which she finds mentally difficult to span.

Being a pastor's wife is the most hazardous and heart-breaking occupation that a woman can have. Often she feels that her wedding vows should have included the promise to love, honor, and obey every member of her husband's congregation. At times she is convinced she married a church.

The pastor's wife is expected to practice more than her husband preaches. Many must make perfect homes, raise perfect children, live perfect lives, and do it on less than living wages and often without the love or understanding of the members of the flock.

By far the greatest suffering of the pastor's wife comes from those hidden feelings within her that cannot be expressed to others. It is not from external work, or difficulties encountered, or the sacrifices made, but from the things she senses and sees. Many a pastor's wife may smile with poise and dignity upon the people of her husband's pastorate, and all the while be covering the hurt of the broken heart she carries.

Let it not be thought that the pastor's wife is less dedicated than her husband. Often she is giving every ounce of strength to the Lord's work, only to be pushed beyond her endurance by thoughtless church members. Probably there has never been a pastor's wife who has not at times dissolved into tears, convinced she can take the pressure no longer. At such times she believes all she has ever done has been in vain. While in the throes of such tumult, the straw bends to the breaking point, and she often finds herself suggesting to her husband that surely there is another aspect of the Lord's work they could do, where they might be happier and more appreciated. Belittle her not, for she will rally and rise from her knees to dry her eyes and stand by her preacher's side with renewed efforts.

Think of Noah's wife. She was the wife of the only preacher that God had in the days when a wicked world was staggering on to its doom. She stood faithfully by her preacher-husband though he was often crushed by the futility of his ministry to a world which had forgotten God. Together they faced the scorn and contempt of one hundred and twenty years of ministry to a world that stopped its ears to God's Word. Through it all she stood true to her husband and her God. She was some woman! When God destroyed this world, her boys were the only boys worth saving (the sons of a preacher!). She rode the storm and flood with no word of complaint, though her home was an unsettled relationship with a stinking zoo. She lived, as it were, in two worlds. She stood true to God in the new world though Noah came to shame.

There was a time when the greatest person in the world was a preacher's wife, and, if we could have the scales removed from our eyes to see things aright, we would find it is still that way. The wife of the preacher belongs to that blest company of whom it is said, the world is not worthy.

18 SCHOLAR AND STUDENT

The preacher who learns how to study and develop the Word of God will always have freshness and variety and will not wear out. This is one of the secrets of long and fruitful pastorates. Dig deep into the great gold mines of the Word, continually bringing forth things new and old, and keep the mental appetites of the people keen for fresh food from God.

It is a disgrace for a preacher to wear out in a few months; for the mine of truth from which he can draw is inexhaustible. No preacher was ever great enough to exhaust the vast range and fathomless depths of revealed truth. The Bible is the world's book. It speaks appropriately and with authority to the people of every age and race and clime.

Talk about Texts, and Themes, and Messages! There are great doctrines to preach in all their glory and fullness; great personalities to resurrect from the graves of the dim past and make them live before our eyes and inspire our drooping spirits; great historic lessons to draw from other days and dead nations which are especially needed by our age so sick with the awful malady of wealth and worldliness, and forgetfulness of God. There are great orations calculated to thrill our hearts; great poems to move our sensibilities and quicken our souls; great confessions of national and personal sins which ought to be repeated today; great prayers to lift from our contrite hearts. There is no heart or need this Book cannot touch and answer.

Lack of study makes the approaching Lord's day a dread. Like the pastor who would send the eyes of his imagination roving over the thin little patch from which he had gleaned so constantly, filled with doleful wonder as to where he should gather a few more ears of corn for next week's bread. He has no barns, or, if he has, they are empty! If we cultivate big farms we shall have well stocked barns.

How are we to preach about Amos unless we live with him on the hills of Tekoa, become part of his surroundings, go with him into Bethel, and listen to the beat of his holy heart? How can we enter into the teaching of Hosea, unless by the power of a vividly exercised imagination we recover his surroundings? We must captivate the sights and sounds and scents of his book. Or how are we going to preach about the Lord's tender ministries unless we can get into the leper's skin, and look out through his darkened windows, and shrink with his timidity, or come running with him along the highway, and in his very person kneel before the Lord. We must see that man, hear him, feel him, be him.

Be patient in your study of the Word. It often takes time for a good sermon to ripen for use. The weakness of smaller preachers is that their time is "always ready": the mighty preachers have long seasons when they know their time "is not yet come." They can keep the message back, sometimes for years, until some day there is a soul in it, and a movement about it, which tells them "the hour is come." Beware of the facility which, if given a day's notice, is ready to preach on anything. Let patience have her perfect work. Preparation is a long process: the best sermons are not made, they grow.

When you have discovered a jewel, give it a most appropriate setting. When you have discovered a truth, give it the noblest expression you can find.

Paul admonished Timothy to "give attendance to reading." The closet of prayer has been called the minister's Holy of Holies; and his study the "Holy Place" where his mind is trained to keep even step with his Spirit-filled heart. Prayer and study go hand in hand.

He who accepts the call to the ministry should understand that by that act he dedicates himself to a lifelong studentship, without a college vacation. Death alone can grant the graduating diploma.

The pastor wrongs himself who does not study. What is tedious first will afterward be pleasant. There is no other way, else you will ever be a trifler all your days, and a petty, superficial teacher. Jesus charged Peter to "FEED my lambs," not starve them.

A power with people seven days in the week, and fifty-two weeks in the year, and several years in succession, does not come without sweat of brain and intense mental application. An empty-headed, pretty, dapper, little fox may be a social success for a season; a lodge-joining, wire-pulling, joking-jigger for Jesus may go on for awhile without brains or sense; but it takes a real man with trained mind and heart to gather and hold for a generation a congregation of men by the preaching of "Christ and Him crucified."

FEED the sheep. Men are hungry for the Bread of Life. It is mean and contemptible to thrash old straw and deliver chaff to the poor, starving multitudes. The pastor must gather manna daily. He must break and distribute to the hungry multitudes the loaves which his Lord has blessed.

Charles Spurgeon had an academy course but never went to college. His private study was his only university, and his professors were the books he read. Yet few men, if any, ever sent more material to press, or were so much read or quoted.

The Holy Spirit simply will not sanction mental indolence nor endorse the needless ignorance of a minister who, in this age of schools, books, and opportunities, is too lazy to study and learn.

Spirituality and intellectuality are not necessarily opposed to each other. William Carey was an English cobbler who acquired only the rudiments of the common school, but read, read, read. He was still a cobbler at age twenty-eight, but in his thirty-third year landed in India, the first modern English missionary! He became the most learned scholar and Bible translator of all the missionaries of Christian history. He translated the Bible into thirty-six languages of India. When complimented about it in his old age he said, "There is nothing remarkable about it; I have no genius, but I can plod. I can persevere in any definite pursuit."

19 COMFORTER AND COUNSELOR

Medical men set forth the proposition that sickly people are often greatly helped in their appetites and attitudes simply by a frequent change of the ware on which their food is served. And so it is with the ministry of the Word of God. Put the old truth to human hearts in a fresh way.

According to the patriarch Job, every man is "born unto trouble." That includes every member of our flock. Therefore it is imperative and inevitable that we leave our pulpits on the sacred quest of seeking out the individual needing personal attention. Unshared trouble can bring on physical ailments and premature age. What then can we do to help the troubled? Often we find that all someone requires is a sympathetic audience. It is not that he needs our exhortation, but our ears.

Often the need of people is just to talk to someone; for a fear shared is frequently a fear destroyed. Being the silent partner allows us to see the mysterious workings of God's grace and the yoke being made easy and the burden light. Oh, how great and needful is the ministry of spiritual comfort and counsel. How superb is the ministry of that servant who is filled with the Wisdom and Word of God. He is "able to comfort them which are in any trouble" (II Cor. 1:4).

Never forget the importance of the individual touch. The Good Shepherd left the ninety and nine to help ONE poor wandering sheep. Dare we do less than give our personal attention? A preacher who is not in contact with his people in their sufferings and sorrows misses one of the great means of learning how to speak to them with effect. He enters the depths to be with the discouraged and depressed; he goes to the chamber of death to help the dying, and often receives more than he gives. The teacher becomes the taught.

Spurgeon put it well when he said, "Be much at death-beds; they are illuminated books. What splendid gems are washed up by the waves of Jordan! What fair flowers grow on its banks! The everlasting fountains in the glory land throw their spray aloft and the dewdrops fall on this side the narrow stream. While the departing sit in the suburbs of the New Jerusalem, God whispers in their ears and they tell us a little of what the Spirit has revealed. I will part with all my books, if I may see the Lord's Elijahs mount their chariots of fire."

Near the end of his fruitful life Ian Maclaren declared that if he could begin his ministry over again he would strike the note of comfort far oftener than he had done. We do well to remember that the amount of trouble in the average congregation is far greater than an unimaginative onlooker would possibly guess. As long as God sets His image on the soul, and as long as men are restless till they rest in Him, so long will the preacher's task persist. Like our Lord, we have been sent into this tear-filled Valley of Baca to "heal the broken-hearted."

Even the man blind from his birth can see that this is a world of broken hearts, broken homes, and broken hopes. Sin has broken through the wall of Paradise and a herd of woes has come in upon us, trampling down everything fair and beautiful. Fallen man found a sword at the very gate of Eden, and he finds a waiting sword at every gate. In an effort to alleviate the hurt of humanity and to offer guidance and comfort, many have turned to the wisdom of this world and to the flood of writings on Psychiatry and Counseling. It seems the consolations of God have become small (Job 15:11) and the Word of God secondary. While there may be avenues of alleviation with merit, ours is a ministry of the Word of God. And it is second to none!

What ministry can take the place of lifting the head of the fallen and fainting to let them catch a breath of the fragrance of the heather from the hills of Home; or to remind the lonesome of the innumerable hosts of immortals ready to welcome them into eternal companionship; or to point out to the bereft soul that there is no death in the celestial country, that no gravedigger's spade will cleave the sacred soil there!

Is there a ministry greater than that of bringing hope to the dying sinner; declaring with a "thus saith the Lord" that his sins can be covered, that the blood of God's dear Son goes deeper than the stain has gone! Is there a greater joy than establishing hearts in the Faith, assuring them that heaven is at our very doorstep, that the resplendent river of God's Grace, deep and wide as the joys of heaven, flows on amid the balm and brightness of skies roseate with gladness, and that not a tear of man mingles with those pure waters there!

The man of God can become thoroughly furnished unto every good work. He can know the joy of sharing comfort and counsel, for he serves the God of all comfort whose name is both Wonderful and Counsellor (Isa. 9:6).

20 CHURCHES AND CHANGES

It is frightening the way some determine the direction the will of God is leading them. John Newton thought that neither the opening of the Bible at a venture, nor the sudden impression of a text, nor special freedom in prayer over a matter, nor a timely dream, furnished any reliable direction. The Lord rather opens and shuts, throws down walls of difficulty, or hedges the way with thorns, for those who confidently seek His guidance by prayer. They know that their concerns are in His hands and they fear to run before He sends, or to delay when He directs an advance.

When an affluent pastorate becomes vacant, usually there are scores of recommendations or personal applications for the position. However, a pulpit committee often takes months searching for a man whom the church desires for its pastor. The reason being that they are looking for a man of God with a message from God, a man with Urim and Thummin, a man whose heart is ablaze with spiritual zest and knowledge. A congregation will overlook some deficiencies and even some faults in a pastor if only he is a good preacher, with God's message.

Should a pastor resign without another work to go to? Wisdom suggests that this be answered from an aeronautical viewpoint: it is better never to jump without a parachute! Bread cast upon the waters will return after many days, and we do well to remember the word "many."

If no door of ministry opens immediately, don't give up. The great Bible scholar Marcus Dods waited for six years before a church would call him! During that time he preached, studied, mastered the Word, and waited God's time. When the door finally opened, it led into a lifetime of fruitful service.

Sometimes a change is needed, and the desire for it is legitimate. It is not that the laborer looks for an escape from his calling; but some personal crisis may arise, a health problem may occur with a member of the family, or a situation become more unbearable in his ministry, either of which may necessitate the change. God understands and often sees fit to lead us into another location or sphere of work.

Though we pray earnestly and seek a change in our area of ministry, God may choose temporarily to keep all doors closed to us. Remember, God hung the world on nothing and He may see fit to keep us hanging in thin air for awhile. Our hearts may grow weary when nothing seems to "open up" and we continue to labor under a burdensome load, wondering why God doesn't do something. But we must not be weary (lose heart) in well doing, for in due season we shall reap if we faint not, and it is this extended view that sustains us most.

God is in the Door business. He closes doors as well as opens them. Even Paul knew what it was to have doors of seeming great opportunity closed to him (Acts 16:6-7). He found out that the door which God opened in Philippi was better and more profitable than would have been any door his hand had opened. When the Holy Spirit closes a door before us we can give a hearty Amen and thank Him for the beauty, the sweetness, and the fragrance of His ministry of hindrance. He is the Hinderer as well as the Helper. Even God's hindrances are fraught with the graces of His heavenly touch. We may come to closed doors in our ministry only to find the locks dripping with sweet smelling myrrh as our Lord leaves evidences that He has already been there.

To the faithful of Philadelphia our Lord revealed Himself as the One Who openeth, and no man shutteth; and shutteth, and no man openeth (Rev. 3:7). One of the most difficult lessons for us to learn is to wait patiently upon Him Who opens and closes doors, and be content with our state and His timing. While we wait we soon find that the pressures of this rushing generation exhausts our store of endurance, and we wonder whether our patience will survive our situation or the prolonged test.

Paul survived such a waiting test despite a multitude of changes and unexpected hindrances. His heart's desire seemed fulfilled when he finally set sail on a journey that fitted both his aims and ambitions; but it was also a journey that was part of the purpose and plan of God for him. Because God had promised he would bear witness in Rome, Paul began his voyage eager and confident that his arrival in Rome would soon be a reality. Yet on that important divinely-planned course, God's great preacher "SAILED SLOWLY MANY DAYS" (Acts 27:7). Contrary winds swept down across the deep, impeding his progress and making it impossible to pursue a straight course. At times it appeared as though Paul would never reach Rome.

Most of us find that our holiest desires and our highest ambitions are reached and realized only after long, painful waiting. Though we pray for God's leading and blessing, and feel that we are going in the direction of His will, things move so slowly at times. We find it hard to be patient when our Lord permits contrary winds to thwart the course and progress of our ship. Restlessness sets in. We become fretful and impatient with the unhurried steps of Sovereignty. We find difficulty in accepting the will of God to "SAIL SLOWLY MANY DAYS." Though the course set before us may involve many changes, rest assured that God is ever on time regarding His schedule, and He will see that we reach our Rome on time.

21 VITALITY AND VISION

How sensitive is the organ of spiritual perception, and how vigilantly it has to be guarded if the preacher is to retain his vitality in and his vision of the deeper things of God. One may find in his ministry that an evil temper can make him blind to spiritual things. He may find that jealousy can scale his eyes until the heavens give no light. He may find that paltry things can raise an earth-born cloud between himself and the hills of God. He may find when he enters his study that his moral and spiritual condition demands his first attention. The heavens may have become as brass! The Gospel of John may appear as a wilderness without verdure or dew! He may find that when his spirit is impaired, his Bible and books are only like so many spectacles behind which there are no eyes; he has no sight!

The only sure guarantee to maintain spiritual perception and power is to set the Lord always before us. That makes all the difference. We know we can endure all things if we see Him who is invisible; and we must see Him if our people are to see Him. We are charged to preach Christ, but the immensity of that charge staggers us. It defies any attempt of mortal man. To describe this Eternal One, this Rose of Sharon, this Lily of the Valley, is like standing by the ocean shore with the impossible task of dipping the ocean dry a handful at a time. It is like wading into the sea of His sublime beauty, filling our hands with adjectives and then wading ashore and pouring them out in an attempt to properly portray the One who is altogether lovely, and then plunging once again into that unfathomable sea, while all the time that ocean seems to grow larger and larger and our hands smaller and smaller.

See Him we must, yet there is no mortal mind in any race or realm possessing the capacity to describe or the capability to declare the glories of the Son of God. His might and His majesty are utterly inconceivable. Solomon said, "The heaven and the heaven of heavens cannot contain thee" (I Kings 8:27).

We may search literature and lexicons, encyclicals and encyclopedias only to discover the inadequacy of the languages of men; He is beyond "words." He is indeed the "unspeakable" gift. Artists cannot depict Him, poets cannot describe Him, bankers cannot evaluate Him, Earth cannot equal Him, and the angels of heaven cannot compare with Him. Despite it all, we can "See Him."

If the man of God is to accomplish the abiding, he must see the permanent, the everlasting, the invisible. He must look, not with his eyes, but with his soul. Like Moses, he must endure as seeing Him who is invisible. Moses looked with his eyes and saw Egypt, its power, its wealth, its spendor, and himself as the heir apparent to its throne. An ordinary man would have looked no further. The "seen" would have been good enough, but Moses looked beyond Egypt to the kingdom that was coming; and he saw HIM, the invisible God whose throne was eternal and whose authority was supreme. As he saw the unseen, his heart beat faster, and he refused the immediate for the imperishable. That vision stiffened his courage. He walked out of the palace, threw down worldly ambition, and setting his face toward the desert, began a lifelong ministry in which he endured because he SAW HIM who is invisible.

Moses had taken the look that lasted. It was the look that gave him permanent vision and vitality. The divine record (Deut. 34:7), when speaking of Moses at the end of his earthly ministry, said, "His eye was not dim" (there is his VISION), "nor his natural force abated" (there is his VITALITY). The vision is mentioned first, for it was the vision which gave Moses the vitality.

The combined powers of this world were no match for this simple shepherd with nothing but a rod in his hand and a vision in his heart. Moses had seen what Pharoah had not seen, and so he endured. It was SEEING HIM that made the difference. That vision of the Invisible made Moses the creator of a civilization, the leader of a nation, the shepherd of a people. It is that vision which enables the man of God to endure all things, and to keep on walking by faith.

22 PRESENT AND PROSPECT

Men of God have soon found that preaching is not always popular; that more often it is perilous. Natural man does not appreciate hearing that spoken Word which removes the mask of morality and exposes the way of life contrary to the righteousness of God. In Old Testament times the false prophets, priests, plutocrats, and potentates turned bitter against those who came preaching personal and national accountability to God. Tradition says Isaiah was sawn asunder, Jeremiah suffered untold vilification, Amos was driven from Israel by Amaziah the priest of Bethel, and John the Baptist was imprisoned and ultimately beheaded.

This godless world has not changed for the better, and it remains that it requires conviction, character, courage, and commitment to preach to a wicked generation desirous of preserving their status quo and living in rebellion to the Most High God. One may be threatened like Peter, imprisoned like Paul, banished like Chrysostom, martyred like Savanarola, excommunicated like Luther, refused the use of pulpits like John Wesley, or be the victim of jealousy like multiplied numbers of successful preachers.

It takes conviction to hold forth the truth when the times disregard it. It takes character to keep on serving faithfully when others are leaving their pulpits fed up with apathy and mistreatment of those they serve. It takes courage to serve a congregation when you have to hold the lid on things with one hand and at the same time push things forward with the other; when noisesome critics and fault-finders crawl out of the woodwork to lift their voices against you, and the inactives show up to harmonize in the chorus. It takes commitment when you have no security in sight, your health swiftly fading, and your wife in constant tears over your continued crucifixion.

Perhaps God has called some to go through the fiery furnace made seven times hotter, or by hell's conspiracy have been forced by wicked hands into the den of hungry lions. Perhaps when there seemed no adequate explanation, and the heavy heart cried out for an answer, the precious Spirit of God caused the eye of faith to see beyond the present to the prospect, and there was given a revelation instead of an explanation. The spirit and soul revived to say, "Let sickness come, let poverty come, let sorrows come, let storms assail, let all hell move against us, NOW we see through a glass darkly, BUT THEN face to face; NOW I know in part BUT THEN shall I know even as also I am known!"

We have such a revelation! Though the shadows lengthen, and the long night sets in, and though the feet of our children walk bare on the ground, and though their stomachs are empty and the cupboards destitute, and though friends have forsaken us and the fiery darts are hurled from all sides, and though ten thousand criticisms are lofted against us, and the poisoned dagger has entered our back, "WE KNOW that all things work together for good to them that love God, to them who are the called according to His purpose!"

Is it worth it? Is it worth continuing to labor when there seems to be no result; to keep on ministering when it appears nothing is being lastingly accomplished; to go on living by truth when a lie looks to be master of the day? Is it worth putting toil and seed into soil that remains barren and unresponsive? Yes, it is worth it, for that is well doing!

It is worth it all in this present life, and it will be worth it all in the life to come. It was worth it for those who served before us, and it will be worth it for those who may serve after us. It will be worth it for those servants of God to whom the world gave the cold shoulder, called the offscouring of all things, and begrudged the least recognition. It will be worth it for those who fought on, weary and worn, beside the brook Besor. Who kept on when they didn't feel like going on. Who stuck to duty through headache and heartache. Who stayed faithful in the commonplace, laboring often undistinguished and obscure. It will indeed be worth it all for the day of recompense and reward is soon coming when the all-glorious Son of David shall personally distribute among us the kingly garlands of glory, the unfading crowns, the shining scepters, the thrones and the kingdoms. It is worth it for we know that our labor is not in vain in the Lord!

Let us then be steadfast, unmoveable, always abounding in the work of the Lord. Let us not forget the wonderful ways in which God has wrought for us great victories on the field of battle. Like Samuel at Mizeph let us raise our Ebenezer and declare, "Hitherto hath the Lord helped us."

It will be but awhile and we shall stand on Jordan's near shore and look back upon our life of service, like Moses when he stood on Nebo's lonely heights and viewed the land of Promise and said farewell forever to the wilderness. May we be able to sum it all up on that day, as did the apostle Paul where he thought back upon the most memorable thirty years of ministry that any human being has ever been privileged to experience, and say,"I have fought a good fight, henceforth there is laid up for me a crown of righteousness, which the Lord the righteous Judge, shall give me."

Let us go on with that vision of Better Things before us, encouraged onward by that immortal cloud of witnesses, the illustrious company of the holy with whom by God's grace we are numbered. Our prospects are growing more glorious! This present world can be endured—it is but our trial with the transient. We are almost done with it. However, "Our light affliction, which is but for a moment, worketh for us a far more exceeding and eternal weight of glory."

What are temporary toils and trials, and brief battles with the bulls of Bashan, when weighed against the pleasures forevermore at God's right hand? One moment in the presence of Him Who has called us with a Holy calling will more than compensate for the inconveniences and impediments of the passing present.

Let us then lay aside all the unnecessary, and preach! Preach the Word! Preach the Cross and Christ! Preach faithfully in season and out! Preach on and on, "Looking unto Jesus the Author and Finisher of our faith; Who for the JOY . . . ENDURED . . !"

BIBLIOGRAPHY

Baxter, Richard. The Reformed Pastor. John Knox
    Press: Richmond, Virginia, 1956.

Beecher, Henry Ward. Yale Lectures On Preaching.
Fords, Howard, and Hulbert: New York, 1881.

Bitting, William G. The Teaching Pastor. Judson
Press: Philadelphia, 1923.

Brooks, Phillips. Lectures On Preaching. Dutton:
New York, 1877.

Chapman, J. Wilbur. The Problems Of The Work.
    Hodder and Stoughton: New York, 1911.

Dale, R. W. Nine Lectures On Preaching. Barnes:
New York, 1878.

Gladden, Washington. The Christian Pastor. Charles
Scribner's Sons: New York, 1910.

Hills, A. M. Homiletics and Pastoral Theology.
Nazarene Publishing House: Kansas City, MO,
1929.

Jowett, J. H. The Preacher, His Life And Work. Abingdon
    Press: New York, 1912.

Kern, John A. The Ministry To The Congregation. Methodist Publishing House: Nashville, 1912.

Leavell, Roland G. Prophetic Preaching. Baker Book House: Grand Rapids, 1963.

Lloyd-Jones, D. Martyn. Preaching and Preachers. Zondervan: Grand Rapids, 1972.

McDowell, William F. Good Ministers of Jesus Christ. Yale Lectures. Abingdon Press: New York, 1917.

Quayle, William A. The Pastor-Preacher. Eaton and Means: New York, 1910.

Riley, William B. The Preacher And His Preaching. Sword Of The Lord Publishers: Wheaton, 1948.

Robertson, A. T. The Glory Of The Ministry. Revell: New York, 1911.

Shaw, S. B. Old Time Religion. S. B. Shaw, Publisher: Chicago, 1904.

Spurgeon, C. H. Lectures To My Students. Zondervan: Grand Rapids, 1955.

Tucker, William Jewett. The Making And The Unmaking Of The Preacher. Houghton Mifflin: Boston, 1898.

Weisberger, Bernard A. They Gathered At The River. Little, Brown and Company: Boston, 1958.

Wiersbe, Warren. Walking With The Giants. Baker Book
    House: Grand Rapids, 1955.

Whyte, Alexander. Whyte's Bible Characters. Vol. I and
II. Zondervan: Grand Rapids, 1953.

Whyte, Alexander. Treasury Of Alexander Whyte. Edited
    by Ralph G. Turnbull. Revell: Westwood, NJ, 1963.

Keith E. Knauss wrote out of the experiences and years of a full pastoral and educational background. He held five degrees, having graduated from Practical Bible Training School, Vennard College, Oakland University, and Burton College and Seminary.

Books by Keith E. Knauss:

The Shadow Of Salvation
Manifestation Of Messiah (Commentary on Revelation)
Moments With Messiah
Musing Of Messiah (Commentary on Isaiah)
O Thou Man Of God
Perfect Peace
Putting Music To The Words
Where Is The King?
Travelogues In Truth

Editors note: Brother Knauss had a unigue writing style. We would like to reprint his other titles. If you are in possession of one of the above titles, please contact us at the address on the facing page.

Initially, this book was published by the *Fundamental Baptist Fellowhip of America.* Today, this fellowship is better known as the *Fundamental Baptist Fellowship International.*

The Mission Statement of the FBFI reads:
The Fundamental Baptist Fellowship International exists to provide a rallying point for Fundamental Baptists seeking personal revival and the opportunity to work with committed Bible-believers in glorifying God through the uncompromising fulfillment of the Great Commission.

The official organ of the FBFI is: *Frontline Magazine*

FBFI Contact Information:
2801 Wade Hampton Blvd.
Suite 115-165
Taylors, SC 29687
864.268.0777
800.376.6856
info@fbfi.org

Faithful Life Publishers would like to thank the FBFI for their confidence in letting us reprint *Heartbeats of the Holy.* FLP is an independent Christian company that is striving to bring challenging works, both new and old, to fundamental Baptist believers. FLP titles are available for purchase at Christian bookstores across the country and/or our website, www.FLPublishers.com.

A portion of the sales from this book will go
toward the FBFI, to be used at their discretion.

Faithful Life Publishers
3335 Galaxy Way
North Fort Myers, FL 33903
239.652.0135
888.720.0950
www.FLPublishers.com
info@FLPublishers.com